Experts Writing Academy's

The Ultimate Guide to

Writing, Publishing & Marketing

Your Book.

Laura J. Kendall, CPC

Laura J. Kendall is the author of over 19 books, a certified professional writing & publishing coach and Founder of Experts Writing Academy.

Visit her at:

www.expertswritingacademy.com

www.authorlaurajkendall.com

Join our online training for writers at

http://expertswritingacademy.mykajabi.com

Contents

Chapter 1: Success stories.

Chapter 2:The Writer's Mindset: Discovering Your Compelling Why.

Chapter 3: Discovering Your Inner Dream Squasher.

Chapter 4: What is stopping you?

Chapter 5: Your Writing Style.

Chapter 6: What will you write?

Chapter 7: Start Writing.

Chapter 8: Formatting

Chapter 9: Non Fiction Writers Section.

Chapter 10: Fiction Writer's Section.

Chapter 11: Publishing Choices and Scams

Chapter 12: Marketing your book:

Chapter 13: Conclusion

Dedication

To all those who dare to bare their souls, share their stories and bring happiness or help to others.

I find it sad when others let their stories die within them. If your story can help just one person or bring happiness as they forget about their troubles for a short while, I believe it is a gift you give when you share it.

Laura J. Kendall

Acknowledgements

I'd like to thank my editor the late Jennifer S. O'Reilly for going over this book with a fine tooth comb and correcting my mistakes and putting a final polish on it. Any mistakes still in this book (like this paragraph she never read) are purely mine to own.

I will miss you Jennifer.

Foreword

My story began in 1993 when I decided to write a murder mystery. To say this was easy would be a wallop of a good lie. The truth is it took me sixteen years to write and publish my first fiction book, "A Simple Case of Suicide."

At the time I started writing, I was in an unhappy marriage and both my parents had recently passed away. I found there was no better way to disappear into another world than writing a novel.

I have always loved reading mystery-suspense books so I thought, "Well how hard can it be to write one?" Well thoughts like that came back to bite me in the old keister.

I found out that writing, especially a suspense novel, was darn hard, and involved extensive plotting, coming up with red herrings, and learning how to show the action rather than tell it.

I started writing before personal computers were on the scene. (Yup that makes me about 29 years old. How's that for some good fiction?)

To this day, I still write a lot of my non- fiction and fiction books longhand in notebooks. I buy a bunch of cheap notepads and keep one with me so I can always write when the mood or sudden plot twist hits. I also keep one by my bed so if an idea hits me in the middle of the night, I can jot it down and go right back to sleep. Once I have enough on paper I type it into a Word document. Having a laptop is awesome as well and as I have grown in my computer skills I find myself typing more and more of my books right into Word.

You will figure out what feels best for you.

I know how difficult it can be to decide on a non-fiction topic, develop fictional characters, plots, settings, and think about your book's formatting. My hope is that this book will save you countless hours of anxiety and frustration during the creation of your masterpiece.

"The greatest danger for most of us is not that our aim is too high and we miss it, but that it is too low and we reach it." Michelangelo

I have to come clean with the reason it took me sixteen years to write and publish my first book. It was because I got too caught up in other people's opinions and didn't value my own enough. I would write a couple of pages and hand them over to whoever would read them and give their opinion. Unfortunately, I took many of the critical opinions to heart and I started to doubt my own abilities. Even though I am still appreciative of all the feedback I receive I now know that the opinion that means the most is my own.

I was so insecure about my writing when I started and this insecurity crippled me so much that I would put my manuscript away for a year at a time, only to take it back out, and try again. This went on for fifteen years until one day I got a big swift kick of encouragement from a friend. I picked up my pen and I haven't put it down since. I just kept saying to myself, "I'm going to get my story down on paper, even if no one ever reads it."

Once I made the decision, "A Simple Case of Suicide" was done within the year. Each book is now easier to write and takes less time. It's amazing what confidence and a "can do" attitude will do!

If a story or book idea keeps coming back to you over and over again it will not go away until it is down on paper or in print. Sharing your story is a gift you give the world!

Self-doubt is the killer of dreams. I encourage you to go for it. I believe in you! Hold on to your dreams and don't let anything or anyone stop you!

If you want to be a writer, I have great news for you! You, my friend, can write and self-publish as many books as you desire. Don't let self-doubt, or the opinions of others kill your dream of being an author, so many famous authors have been rejected, some hundreds of times. One of my favorite mantras is: Face the fear and do it anyway!

As Jack Canfield says, "Don't live someone else's dreams!" I say live your dreams!

We have a private facebook group for our online students. Students can request to join the group at Experts Writing Academy. I'd love to connect with you.

Until then love with an open and accepting heart - starting with yourself first, celebrate your victories no matter how small, and never give up on your dreams.

Happy Writing!

Laura J. Kendall, CPC - Founder of Experts Writing Academy

Chapter One

Success Stories

A few years ago, it was unheard of for a self-published writer to become a successful and mainstream author.

Well, hold onto your hat, because times have changed! Thanks to computers, amazon.com, and the Internet, many self-published writers are becoming huge, and sometimes overnight, successes.

A recent success story is that of E.L.James, who self published a little book you may have heard of titled "Fifty Shades of Grey." After the book went viral on blogs and social media it was picked up by a major publisher for seven figures, a movie has been made, and James is now a reputable mainstream author.

Amanda Hockings, a paranormal fiction writer, is another great success story. Hockings wrote several novels over nine years all of which were rejected by publishers. One April day in 2010 she decided on a whim to digitally upload her books on amazon.com. Within six months she sold 150,000 copies of her books. Her book sales are now in the millions and growing right along with her bank account, and she did it all without the help of an agent or publishing house!

Michael Prescott has gained recognition, success, and critical praise for twenty books he wrote over thirty years. Then came the overwhelming rejection by agents and publishers of his latest thriller, "Riptide." Prescott thought for sure his dreams, career, and success were over. Then he decided to self publish "Riptide" as an eBook. He priced it at 99 cents and sold over 800,000 digital copies! How's that for success?

They are among many self-published authors successfully selling their books as eBooks.

The days of practically having to give up your first born to get an agent or publishing house to even read your book are over. Today authors can take control of their careers through self publishing. While not the norm, some do get noticed by big publishing houses, and are offered lucrative deals. It can happen for anyone of us now that self publishing in paperback or eBook is no longer frowned upon. I get excited each time I hear that an indie author has been discovered and is successfully growing their authorship and career.

To date, I have written and published over 19 fiction and non-fiction books so I know that if I can do it - you can too!

Chapter Two

The Writer's Mindset: Discovering Your Compelling Why.

Mindset is everything when writing a book and the biggest challenge to overcome. One of the best ways to solidify your mindset is to discover your compelling why.

To become a published writer, you must have a compelling reason to take this journey.

Some questions to think about are:

1. Why do you want to write a book?

2. What actions are you willing to take to make it happen?

3. What might be getting in the way?

What is your reason for writing your book?

1. See your name on the cover?

2. Be a published author?

3. Help someone survive or overcome a situation you did?

4. Create a family heirloom for future generations?

5. Create an ultimate business card that you will give to prospective clients?

6. Have your book go viral and become an instant overnight sensation and millionaire?

7. See the story that has been swirling around in your mind, finally down on paper?

8. Leave a lasting legacy for generations to come?

9. Teach readers your expertise in a step by step or how to book?

These are just a few examples of compelling reasons to write a book.

Why do you want to write a book? Write it down and own it! Once you do, nothing and no one will stop you from achieving it! Writing can be frustrating and lonely at times. To write a book is to decide against all odds that you will complete it and publish it!

People inspire you, or they drain you - pick them wisely.
-Han F. Hansen

There will be many well-meaning and some not-so-well meaning people along your journey. Stay true to yourself and follow your heart. Not the opinions of others!

Surround yourself with people who support you and your dream. Keep these gems close. Remember, when others put you down or mock you, it is never about you. It is always about them, their insecurities, self doubt, self hatred, or jealousy. They are the ones who have no vision.

"You have to believe in yourself when no one else does. That's what makes you a winner." Venus Williams

Exercise One

State Your Compelling Why:

The top three reasons I want to write a book are:

1.

2.

3.

From your list, what is your top reason for writing your book? A reason that is so compelling that nothing will stop you! Write it below.

My Number One Compelling Reason Or Why is:

Now on the flip side there may be something or someone stopping you from following through.

The next exercises will help you discover what may be stopping you.

Chapter Three

DISCOVERING YOUR INNER DREAM SQUASHER

Discovering your Inner Dream Squasher is one of the most empowering things you will ever do for yourself.

What is an Inner Dream Squasher (IDS)? - An IDS is that negative voice or inner critic that each of us has deep inside, controlling our thoughts, self esteem, actions, beliefs, and what we feel we deserve in life, or can accomplish in life.

My IDS controlled every aspect of my life for most of it. It wasn't until my late 40's I finally started realizing this, learning about my IDS and taking control.

Inner Dream Squashes believe it or not are given to us when we are very young by parents, friends, boyfriends, girlfriends, teachers, strangers or a traumatic event.

Things we are told about ourselves we take in as very real, start to believe and begin living our lives accordingly.

Sometimes people are able to pinpoint the exact event that fixated this inner critic into their brain. When parents, friends, and authority figures started telling you negative things about yourself and you started believing them, you started growing a deep seated inner critic/IDS.

Your inner critic can tell you lots of things to believe about yourself.

I'm not good enough

I'm not pretty enough

I'm not thin enough

I'm too fat

I'm not worthy

I'm not smart enough

No one is ever going to love me.

The list could and does go on and on.

I ask you now to really think back and explore your life. Do you have an inner critic hanging on your back that is directing your every move, your thoughts and life?

This critic can develop and take root when people and events happen to you that you have no control over.

Did kids make fun of you at school?

Did a teacher ridicule you in front of the class? (Yup)

Were you made fun of for being different? (Yup)

Did your mother make you feel unacceptable? That no matter what you did or how hard you tried you were never good enough? (Yup)

Did your father make you feel unacceptable? That no matter what you did or how hard you tried you were never good enough?

Were you told you were shy?

Were you told you were stupid?

Were you told that you weren't good enough in any way?

Our Inner Dream Squashers start being engrained early on in life and are born from the words of others and the labels they attach to us.

We all come into this world like blank slates and the people in our lives start painting THEIR words on us as soon as we are born. THEIR words soon become part of our very being. We become what they tell us we are and we soon live up to THEIR words.

It took me until I was 49 years old to truly realize that these words were THEIRS! Well, who the heck are they? Who is anyone to tell me who I am?

The only person who has any say over ME is ME!

When you (like me) finally figure this out it can be a heady and freeing thing. Now don't get me wrong it is not that it will immediately free your mind of all this crap given to you by other people. Not that suddenly you totally come into your own power and totally believe and love yourself right away. No, you have to do some serious work and if you are like me, get some coaching or therapy.

Discovering your Inner Dream Squashers can open a new world for you.

Let's get to work Discovering your Inner Dream Squasher. Many of us have more than one.

Mine was the "I'm not good enough" Inner Dream Squasher.

Naming your Inner Dream Squasher Exercise

1. What is your Inner Dream Squasher/Inner Critic?

2. When was it first created or given to you and by whom?

3. What is the message your Inner Dream Squasher has been telling you about yourself all these years?

4. What is the truth?

5. What do you believe is your Inner Dream Squashers reason for being here?

Naming your Inner Dream Squasher Exercise

When you look deeply at your Inner Critic what is a name that immediately comes to mind? (Try not to name it after a person you know!)

I named my Inner Dream Squasher - THE BLOB. It came to me one night as I was looking at a lava light. This big black blob was moving all over the lamp and into every area. I said wow! That is just like how I've let my Inner Critic infiltrate every area of my life.

Next I found an object (you can make one) that represented my IDS - THE BLOB. It was pretty funny because the only thing I could find to really represent it was a big fake squishy piece of poop from a game store.

What physically represents your Inner Dream Squasher? Start looking around and find an object that represents your IDS in a physical sense.

Discovering your IDS can elicit a whole lot of emotions and feelings. I know I was mad, angry, sad, hurt, and pissed at myself initially. However, as I went through the coaching, training, and process, I came to learn that my IDS was actually protecting me.

Protecting you? How can that be? Well many years ago when you were hurt or belittled your Inner Dream Squasher stepped up to the plate and said, "Oh no, you will never be hurt like that again!"

So, it went about your life making sure you were protected by putting up walls, cutting you off from others, sinking into shyness, using anger so others can't get close. There are so many ways it may have set you up to not get hurt.

Because this is such a powerful process I highly recommend getting therapy or coaching to help you work through this discovery.

Many emotions come to the surface and anger can be misdirected at others whom you perceive as hurting you when you were younger. Don't go it alone!

Please reach out to me if you need me on facebook or at:

expertswritingacademy@gmail.com

You can also find a coach by going to the International Coach Federation link below.

http://www.coachfederation.org/find-a-coach/

What matters most to me is that you know you don't have to go this alone. You matter and so does discovering how to own and reframe your Inner Critic.

What Emotions Are You Feeling Exercise

Emotions can be powerful clues as to what is going on inside of us. No emotion is right or wrong, it simply is. How you are feeling matters and so do you.

With this in mind I'd like you to take a few minutes of quiet time to think about the emotions you are feeling. Sit quietly with your eyes closed if you can and let whatever comes to you come. Write down all the emotions you feel as they start coming to the surface. Just list them and then go back and ask yourself why you are feeling them?

If strong emotions come up in you I highly suggest you reach out to a friend, your coach, or therapist. You do not want to go this alone and you do not have to.

Name your Strengths, Values and Purpose Exercise

Your Inner Critic has actually been helping you grow into the person you are today. It has been your protector as you develop your gifts, strengths, values and life's purpose.

Now we are going to discover your gifts, strengths, and values, and write them down. Discovering your gifts, strengths, and values can help you see what your life's purpose is all about.

Gifts, strengths, and values kind of flow together so where I may classify something as a gift, you may classify it as a value. List whatever feels right to you.

Gifts are abilities we have in life that come naturally or we develop them over time through experience. Gifts flow from us and impact our lives and the lives of others in a positive way.

Example of Gifts

Writing

Publishing

Organizing/Organizer

Trainer

Event Planning/Planner

Sharing

Helping Others

Empowering Others

Coaching

Singing

Playing Music

Teaching

Mentoring

Story Teller

Truly sit and think about all your gifts and then write them down.

My Gifts:

<u>Strengths</u> - Strong characteristics you bring to the table.

Examples of Strengths:

Bravery

Persistence

Hope

Sticktuitiveness

Loyalty

Confidence

Boldness

High Self Esteem

Speaking up or Standing up for those without a voice.

Having an Analytical Mind

Now sit with it and no matter how strange it feels to claim your strengths, be honest and do it. Write them down.

My Strengths:

Values are hugely important and are the basis for which we live our lives. These are the beliefs or ideals you live your life by.

Examples of Values

Authenticity

Commitment

Integrity

Fitness

Judgment

Dependability

Consistency

Feeling Good

Honesty

Kindness

Compassion

There are many others and you can find a list of values at www.expertswritingacademy.com

What values do you live your life by? What do you stand for?

<u>List your top ten values</u>

1.

2.

3.

4.

5.

6.

7.

8.

9.

10.

From the ten values narrow them down to your top five values.

1.	
2.	
3.	
4.	
5.	

From this list of five, pick your most high value. The one you truly want to stand for and live by.

My highest Value is

Now you can see that you have a ton of great qualities. Gifts, Strengths and Values that make you unique. I've learned that perhaps without my IDS I wouldn't have grown to be the person I am today. Perhaps you as well would not have grown into the amazing person you are today without your Inner Dream Squasher's protective stance over your life.

Knowing that your Inner Dream Squasher has really been protecting you from further hurt and pain and you now have the opportunity to see it as your ally.

How would it feel to rename your Inner Dream Squasher and give it new meaning in your life?

It was pretty powerful for me!

<u>Inner Dream Squasher - let's give yours a new name.</u>

Old Name

New Name

<u>Now let's give your newly named IDS a new purpose.</u>

(New Name)_____ I really appreciate you protecting me all these years. I know you did it because you didn't want me to be hurt ever again.

(New Name)_____I've grown and learned a lot through the years. I have many amazing gifts, values and strengths to rely on now and I can take it from here.

Every time your IDS comes up (as it will because this isn't a onetime cure all exercise. Remember your IDS has been protecting you for a long time). Just say again:

(New Name)_____ thank you for protecting me. I can take it from here.

Take a moment and write down anything else would you like to say to your Inner Dream Squasher?

I honor you for taking the time to Discover Your Inner Dream Squasher and the many gifts, strengths and values you have developed. You are an amazing soul on a very interesting journey.

One last thing before you go. Have you discovered your life's purpose yet? That thing that makes you feel empowered and you watch time fly by so fast you didn't remember to even eat lunch.

As I've followed the personal development path of life, I've discovered my life's purpose has changed from that of a paramedic/instructor (although I still practice my value of compassion by working as a paramedic & instructor) to that of an author and publishing coach. I can genuinely say it is very empowering to write and publish a book and to gain the title author.

As a publishing coach, I partner with writers as they go through same process I did as I wrote and published my books. I made a ton of mistakes and spent lots of money I didn't have to by falling for scams. I don't want that to happen to my clients or to you. My mission is to authentically empower other people to know that their story and expertise matters. I want to help them share it with the world. It is truly a gift you give to others when you share your story or expertise. Helping my client's share their story and expertise through a book light me up like nothing else.

I am so grateful for each and every one of you who entrusted me and Experts Writing Academy to partner with you on your writing & publishing journey.

What lights you up? What makes you feel like you are following your true path in life? Discovering your life's purpose will start you down the most amazing life's path. Figure that out and you will be able to start living the life of your dreams.

I stand by ready to offer coaching, accountability, and training in any area you desire as you write and publish your book. You don't have to do it alone. I also highly recommend coaching or therapy as you go through the empowering and sometimes confusing discovery process called life.

This writing exercise is not to replace actual coaching or therapy and is only a small part of the journey. It is highly recommended that if you seek coaching or therapy to guide you through any life changing discovery or event.

Chapter Four

What is stopping you?

Now that you have your compelling reason, let's look at what might be stopping you from following through.

Below list the top three reasons you believe you haven't followed through writing your book.

1.
2.
3.

We all have things that get in the way of following through or believing in ourselves. Mine was my huge inner critic known as the "I'm-not-good-enough gremlin." I let this belief infiltrate every aspect of my life. For sixteen years my inner critic prevented me from writing my first book.

Once you face your own gremlin or inner critic, you can deal with it so it doesn't control your life.

What are three actions steps you can take to overcome what is stopping you from following through and writing your book.

Do you need an accountability partner to keep you on track? Do you need to work with a writing coach? List the action steps you will take below.

The action steps I will take to break through what is stopping me are:

1.
2.
3.

By taking action steps, no matter how small they may be, you are moving forward towards your goal.

I've found that having a coach is one of the most powerful gifts I've ever given myself. Through coaching I have made amazing, positive changes, which is why I went through the training and became a Certified Professional Coach. Now I am beginning to live my dream of helping writers achieve theirs— getting their books published.

Chapter Five

Your Writing Style

Write what you know. Keeping this in mind has made my writing journey fun, challenging, and at times, cathartic.

I write about what I know and I write in my own style. In the beginning, I researched and tried out lots of famous authors styles of writing. In the end, however, my own style fits me best.

Some readers like my style and others don't. That's ok. That's what makes the world go 'round. Learning to not take it personally and to believe in myself continues to be a journey.

What has happened in your life that might make a great story?

What are you passionate about?

What has become so natural to you in life that you can do it without even thinking?

What gets you excited and lights you up inside?

What is the message you want to get out to the world?

Here's some advice: If you base your story on your life and include real people in your book, it's best to get their permission in writing.

You will want to research the legal aspects of using real people, alive, or deceased, in your story. It's a good idea to be familiar with copyright and trademark procedures and laws as well.

Chapter Six

<u>What will you write?</u>

You will need to decide what type of book you are going to write.

A. For non-fiction writers you will need to pick a topic.

  ➤ What are you an expert in? How can you help someone with what you know by sharing it in a book?

  ➤ What type of book will do you want to write? Autobiography, biography, how-to manuals or self-help.

B. For fiction writers you will need to pick a genre.

  ➤ A genre is a classification or type of book you will write. Murder mystery, suspense, and romance are all genres. Readers know what type of story to expect from you based on the genre of the book.

➤ What is your favorite genre? Suspense, thriller, murder mystery, romance, paranormal romance, literary fiction or erotica?

.

Chapter Seven

Start Writing

With the advent of eBooks and Indie Publishing there does not seem to be a set in stone length for a book. In fact the latest findings show that more people enjoy reading shorter books rather that longer.

For reference only I go by these numbers.

Average length of a full length novel is between 60,000 to 120,000 words.

Novella is between 17,000 to 50,000 words.

Short story is below 17,000.

The number of pages these words equal will depend on the font you choose and the size of the font you choose.

Moreover the number of words vary depending on the genre or topic so do your research so you know what to shoot for. I research by going on Amazon.com and search for books in my genre or topic. Then I note their page count.

If you decide to go the mainstream publishing route, know that each publishing house has specific submission requirements. Research the submission requirements before submitting your manuscript to a publisher or publishing house.

Computers make it easy to calculate word and page count no matter what font or format you use.

Viewpoint

From what viewpoint will your character(s) speak?

First person - The main character will use the word "I" and see the world from his or her point of view.

Second person - Second person is used mostly in self-help, do-it-yourself manuals or any book where a narrative style works best. Second person is not used much or if at all in fiction novels.

Third person - The characters speak in "he" or "she" and the reader can see, hear, and feel everything the characters do.

I find it difficult to write in first person. Third person flows more naturally for me. You will discover what feels comfortable for you. It is your story, so if something isn't working it's a good idea to change it.

What are the parts that make up the inside of your book?

I think of my books in five parts:

Title

During the writing process, you need to come up with a working title for your book. This can be both fun and stressful.

A catchy title will draw an audience to your book.

To help title your book, ask yourself some questions:

What is my story about?

Are there any pieces of the plot that stick out in my mind?

What words describe my story?

Start with a working title, which is the title you refer to as you are writing. If it still resonates with you when the book is complete keep it. If not, try another title that works better.

The working title of my book is:

<u>Hook Line:</u> The first line of the novel that grabs your readers and won't let go!

<u>Start thinking about your Hook Line:</u>

The first line of your story must grab the reader. You want to capture the readers' attention so they want to keep reading. This is the line that makes your readers click the "buy" button. It is one of the most important sentences in your book. Take a look at the first lines of the books you most enjoy reading to get some ideas.

A Hook Line to consider for my book is:

<u>Beginning:</u> Introducing your characters, conflict, and plot.

<u>Middle:</u> The middle is the nuts and bolts of the novel. This is where you flesh out your characters and give life to your story line, plot, and conflicts.

<u>End:</u> This is the final chapter of your book. Where you wrap things up or, if it's part of a series, leave an exciting cliff hanger.

Keeping Track Of Your Story

I've tried many ways of keeping track of my characters, the plot, setting, red herrings, etc.

Some writers use outlines, some free-hand, and some use complex charts to keep track of their plots and characters. As I write I keep an outline of what I've written in each chapter. I do the same for future chapters to keep track of plot and character ideas.

For "A Simple Case of Revenge," I kept track of the characters and plot on large poster boards that I hung on the wall. I really like this method and I'll be using the method again for my future novels.

You will eventually come up with what works best for you.

For "A Simple Case of Suicide," I knew the beginning and end right from the start. With my other novels I had a basic idea of the plot, and the characters I learned had minds of their own. I would think they were going one way and wham! Off they went in a another direction. I really find this part of the writing process to be a blast as I never know quite where I'm going. I'm just along for the ride!

Character Profile sheet: I do one of these on each of my characters so I can refer back to it and keep my characters real. This also helped me really get to know my characters inside and out and see them as real people. I know, scary right - smile.

I also do outlines for each chapter so I can make sure my story-line flows and remains consistent. It is very easy to get caught up in writing and forget where you are going. In my novels I have a main plot and a subplot so there is a ton of conflict going on and a variety of characters.

For "A Simple Case of Revenge," I had big pieces of paper tacked to my wall where I hand wrote my story outline, using the chapter by chapter method. This allowed me at a glance to see where I was and where I wanted to go.

Find a way that works for you to keep track of your plot and characters. I made the mistake of trying to follow famous writers and how they wrote. It took me years to find my own way, and now I stick to what feels right to me.

Brainstorming

I love this part of writing! Brainstorming is a process that helps you develop your story or subject. Every book I have written has started with thinking about the story or subject and then brainstorming by writing down anything and everything that comes to mind.

For my fellow mystery/suspense/thriller writers out there you will need to do some extra brainstorming. In this type of genre you will need to introduce some "red herrings" to throw your readers off course and also clues to help them begin figuring out the mystery.

After I brainstorm on paper, I go back and see what fits. Some ideas will work and others won't.

Brainstorming is great if you are feeling anxious about where the plot is going or are experiencing writer's block. For me, brainstorming releases the pressure release and brings the fun back into the writing process.

Editing

If you cannot afford professional editing I suggest you find a friend, relative, or colleague who would be willing to read your book with an editorial eye. Even if they are not professional editors, chances are, a fresh set of eyes will find typos, grammatical errors, and inconsistencies that you will miss.

I do not provide editing services. When I create a paperback or eBook, the client must have had the manuscript already edited.

I once heard a writer say, "Just write and put all the other stuff in later." This has freed up my writing style because I just write and don't worry about editing as I go.

Since I suck at perfect grammar and editing I found that if I focus on this aspect as I write I get distracted and get writer's block. This is why I have my books professionally edited now.

I love feedback and I am grateful to everyone who has taken the time to write reviews on Amazon.com or sent an email to me. While most of my book reviews are overwhelmingly positive, a few readers have said that while they really love the story, they found spelling and grammatical errors. Whenever someone tells me about a specific mistake, I always go back and make the correction. This is very important to be able to establish yourself as a credible author.

Writing a book takes time and many revisions. You will write, rewrite, and edit until you are happy with the final product.

You must decide for yourself how you will tackle the editing aspect.

Chapter Eight

<u>Formatting</u>

You will be formatting both your eBooks and paperback books. In my opinion, eBooks are much easier to format than a paperback book. The formatting you see here is for paperbacks, but usually will work on eBooks as well as long as you take out the extra pages you use to set up your paperback manuscript.

Writer's Tip - My suggestion is that you format your book document before you even start writing. This will save you from doing it after you complete your book and save you time, frustration and headaches. All formatting here is for a Word document since this is what I use to write my books in. This is the formatting that worked for my books, but your books may be different.

Formatting an eBook is very basic, but formatting a paperback for a self-publishing writer can be time consuming and very frustrating until you get the hang of it. It took me much trial and error to format my paperback and eBooks. I found that it depends on the size I choose for the book, the number of pages in the book and the font type I select. Getting your formatting right is a must for producing an excellent quality publication.

If you upload the manuscript yourself on Createspace for a paperback, formatting can be trial and error as well as nerve-wracking. Once you get it down, however, future books are much easier.

Experiment until you find what you like or work with a publishing coach like myself. On the following pages I have listed the formatting I did for a few of my books as a means of reference for you.

Generally I do my eBook first and set up the formatting there as I would for my paperback. The only exception is the extra pages you will be putting in at the beginning to make sure you have a page to autograph as well as having your first chapter page start on the right side of the book. Never forget the autograph page - smile!

The following examples are for your education only and may not work in every situation. Use them as guidelines only and change them to fit your book as you want it to appear.

Formatting your book:

Book Size: 6.69 x 9.61

Formatting for the book you are reading right now - "The Ultimate Guide to Writing, Publishing & Marketing a Book," I used the following:

Font: Palatino Linotype

Font Size: 13

Paper Size: 6.69" x 9.61" (I chose this size because I wanted it to be smaller than workbook size, but big enough to do the writing exercises in.)

Width: 6.69

Height: 9.61

Margins

Top: 0.7

Inside: 0.7

Gutter: 0.11 - note: this is the one you will really have to evaluate in your book. When you go into the online reviewer in Createspace, really look at how the margins for the inside of the book look. This is where the pages go into the binding. You don't your lines of text too close, but you don't want them too far away either. Check out your favorite books and see how their inside text looks in relationship to the binding of the book.

Bottom: 0.7

Outside: 0.7

Gutter position: Left

Portrait

Mirror margins

Apply whole document

Paragraphs & Indents and Spacing

Alignment: justified

Outline Level: body text

Set indentations left & right at zero

Special First line: 0.5

Spacing: Spacing before: 0_Spacing after: 1

(This is what determines the space after each paragraph. You really want to look at this in the preview area below it and see how your lines look and the space between paragraphs look.)

Line Spacing: multiple at 1.3

Each time a chapter ends be sure to put in a page break - do not just hit enter.

Formatting a 6x9 Book

For "The Paramedic Rose Erotic Thriller Series - Book One - A Simple Case of Suicide," I chose.

Font: Cambria

Size Font: 12

Paper Size: 6 x 9.

6 width

9 height

Margins

Top 0.7

Inside 0.11

Gutter 0 .88

Bottom 0.7

Outside 0.8

Gutter position left

Orientation: portrait

Mirror margins

Apply to whole document

Paragraphs & Indents and Spacing

Alignment: justified

Outline: body text

Spacing: Before: 0pt After: 1pt - this is how much space goes between paragraphs. This is another one you will need to look at and see how you like it. You don't want too little space between paragraphs, but you don't want to much either.

Special indent first line: 0.5

Line spacing - Multiple at 1.3 (you can type in the space you want between lines and do not have to use what pops up automatically. Check out the preview box below and see how you like the way the book looks.)

Formatting Tip: Each time you finish a chapter don't just hit enter to go to the next page. You need to insert a page break for Kindle, Kobo and Createspace paperback.

On Barnes & Noble Press they like an actual section break. The good news about the new Barnes & Noble Press is that you can do that on the site itself when you upload your manuscript for each new chapter.

Formatting a 5 x 8 Book

For "A Simple Case of Betrayal - Book Three in The Kendall Rose Erotic Thriller Series", I used the following:

Size: 5x8

Width: 5

Height: 8

Font: Constantia

Font Size: 14

Margins:

Top 0.7

Inside: 0.2

Gutter: 0.75

Bottom: 0.7

Outside: 0.7

Gutter position: left

Portrait

Mirror margins - apply whole document

Paragraphs & Indents and Spacing

Alignment: Left

Outline: body text

Indentations: Left & Right at Zero

Spacing: Spacing Before: 0_Spacing After: 12pt

Special indent first line - 0.25

Line spacing: double

Page Numbers:

Check out your favorite books and you will notice that some do not number the first several pages of the book so that the initial chapter might start anywhere between page 6 - 15. I myself don't inflate my page count and start my initial chapter as page 1.

To insert page numbers can be very time consuming and so this is one of the first things I do before I even start writing. If you decide to let the page count start from the very first page then you will have to set the first chapter page to start as that number page and not show the initial page numbers.

Example if the book has a foreword, dedication, acknowledgment, etc.... these are not numbered, but they count towards the page numbers. So if your chapter starts 6 pages in, then that page number shows as 6.

If you are like me and you want to start your first chapter as page 1, then you will need to put in a section break and set it so no numbers show up or are counted in the acknowledgment, dedication, disclaimer, etc.... and start the page numbers in section two.

Your first chapter should start on the right side of your book so this may mean you have to put in blank pages.

I look at my Word doc and count the first page on left side as a front page and its opposite as a back and so on.

My tip is to look at your favorite books and see how they set up the initial pages.

Paperback Formatting Tips

Experimenting with formatting takes time, but in the end your books will look professional.

The margins will change depending on the width, height, and number of pages.

For page numbering I prefer a bottom footer and always start with a different first page. You may choose something different for your book.

The first chapter page should start on the right side of the book and should be an odd number. You may have to insert blank pages. Take a look at your favorite novel and see how it is done.

If formatting becomes too time consuming, you may choose to pay to have it done. We will format your book for you at Experts Writing Academy.

If you are publishing in paperback, make sure you order a proof book so you can see how the finished product will look.

Chapter Nine

<u>Non Fiction Writers Section</u>

This is for: Experts, coaches, trainers, business owners, overcomers/survivors and anyone who want to leave a lasting legacy

Now you may be thinking; "Well I'm not an expert in anything." I beg to differ as I believe that every one of us is an expert in something. It may not be obvious to you now, but I hope it will be after doing these exercises.

Let's brainstorm together and discover your area of expertise by asking and answering a few questions:

1. What am I an expert in?

2. What can I do that other people ask me for help with?

3. What seems like a no brainer or easy for me to me, but others struggle with?

4. What is my area of expertise? (Coaching, training, speaking, empowering others, addictions.)

5. What have I overcome that can help someone going through a similar situation?

Picking your Book Topic

Answer the following questions honestly.

I am an expert in the following three topics or areas.

1.
2.
3.

Now narrow it down to your number one area of expertise.

A. My Book topic is:

Now I'd like you to think about and write down the answers to the following questions:

B. The problem or problems I will solve for my reader are:

| |
| |
| |
| |
| |
| |
| |
| |

C. I will do this by:

| |
| |
| |
| |
| |
| |

D. My book will help someone who:

Now let's dive deeper into your topic or book subject.

What is your main topic or who is your main subject?

(Ex: If you are writing an autobiography then the subject is yourself.

If you are an expert in something than your topic is the thing you have expertise in.)

| |
| |

What problem or problems do you solve for the reader?

| 1. |
| 2. |
| 3. |
| 4. |

What have you overcome that can help someone dealing with a similar problem or conflict?

| |
| |

.

It is important to know your subject or topic in depth. What would you say to someone who asked you about your topic or subject? Does it flow naturally and completely or do you need to really fine tune it?

Create an individual profile sheet (you can download and print out profile sheets at www.expertswritingacademy.com

Answer the following questions:

1. Area of expertise and why you are an expert in this area:

2. Book Topic:

>

3. My story will help someone with or going through the following:

>
>
>
>

4. My story will help solve the problem or problems of:

>
>
>
>
>
>
>
>
>

5. My topic matters to me because:

| |
| |
| |
| |
| |

6. I want to be remembered for:

| |
| |
| |
| |
| |
| |

7. List your knowledge, experience and qualifications

| |
| |
| |
| |
| |
| |

8. List your professional certifications, degrees or training you have pertaining to your topic:

9. Have you coached, trained, or helped someone in the area of expertise you are writing your book on?

Tip 1: Ask them to write a short review or recommendation of you and if you can then include them in your book, website, cover etc....

Tip 2: Ask them what the top three questions are that they would like to see answered in your book.

10. List all the references you have used to complete your book. Give credit where credit is due.

Non-Fiction Worksheet

Laser Focus

Topic:

Problem or conflict you will solve for the reader:

In a short paragraph answer this question:

The main problem or conflict in my book is _____

and I will solve it by _____.

Now let's figure out what writers or books resonate with you.

My favorite non-fiction books are?

1.

2.

3.

My favorite non-fiction authors are?

1.

2.

3.

Ask yourself the following questions:

1. How did the books make you feel? What emotions did the author's words bring out in you?

2. What is it about their books, stories, or topics, that resonates with you?

3. Why did you buy their books?

4. What problem did their books promise to solve?

5. If it was a how to or self help book, were you clearly and easily able to follow their directions, steps, or call to action?

By understanding your favorite books and their author's writing style you can gain great insight into how you want to approach writing your own book. Emulating your favorite author's writing style can help you as you begin to write your book.

I am by no means saying you should or must write like another writer. In the end you will find your own style of writing and the voice you want to speak from and the voice will be your own.

Not everyone will like your book or writing style and that is ok. In fact it is simply a part of being an author. Learning not to take others words seriously as a reflection of your writing or book is one of the most powerful processes you will go through.

Remember that when you feel insecure (every author does at some point) that you wrote the book on your terms and in your voice and that no one else's words can harm you.

I'll be the first to admit this is one I struggled with initially and still do once in a while. I understand it is easy to say, but sometimes harder to do.

Keep strong in yourself and believe in your book.

Putting it all together - Non- Fiction Book

Working title:

My compelling WHY is:

Subject, topic or area of expertise is:

Viewpoint:

I have overcome:

_____
_____
_____
_____

I am an expert in:

_____
_____
_____

The problem I will solve or help with is:

_____
_____
_____
_____
_____

I will solve it by:

_____

Formatting

Paperback book size:

Font:'

> [blank box]

Font Size:

> [blank box]

Word count:

> [blank box]

Page count:

> [blank box]

Margins:

Top:

Inside:

Gutter:

Bottom:

Outside:

Gutter position:

Portrait

Mirror Margins - Whole Document

Paragraph & Indentations and Spacing:

Alignment:

Outline:

Indentations:

Left:

Right:

Spacing:

Spacing Before:

Spacing After:

Special first line:

Line spacing:

Chapter Ten

Fiction Writer's Section

What's Your Genre?

A genre is a classification, such as murder mystery, romance etc..... Readers know what type of story to expect from your book based on your genre.

My top three genres are:

1.

2.

3.

Now think about which of the genres you listed above is your absolute favorite? Why

My favorite genre is:

Four of my favorite writers from my favorite genre are:

1.

2.

3.

4.

What is it about their stories that resonate with you? How do their stories make you FEEL? What emotions do they bring out in you? Do you disappear into another world for a while?

Understanding why your favorite writers resonate so highly with you can give you great clues as to how you want your writing style to flow. I am by no means saying you should or must write like another writer. You must find your own voice and write in a way that you enjoy. When people read my books they always tell me they can hear my voice in the characters' words. I don't follow anyone else's style because my style is my own. Not everyone will like my style or yours and that's ok. I am proud of my books and you should be super proud of yours too.

Who Are Your Characters?

Protagonist - The main character of the story.

Antagonist - One or more characters who are in conflict with the protagonist.

Supporting characters - These characters add to the story line and have a relationship with the main character.

It is important to know your characters inside and out. I create individual profile sheets for all my characters so I can refer to them as I am writing to ensure consistency throughout the story. Some questions I ask about my characters are:

How old are they?

What kind of car do they drive?

What kind of job do they have?

What do they look like physically? (Height, hair color and length, etc.)

What foods do they like?

Where do they live?

What does their house look like?

What is their sexual orientation?

What kind of pets do they have?

What are their pets' names?

These are just some sample questions for you to consider and expand on. You can create your own questions and answers about your characters.

Once you know your characters and have a detailed description sheet for each one, writing a sequel or series will be a snap!

Worksheet: Character Profile

Name:

Age:

Gender:

Height:

Weight:

Job/title:

Car/truck make and model:

Hair color and length:

Facial hair:

Pet's breed:

Pet's name:

State and town:

Type of house:

Vices:

Best friend:

Hobbies:

Sexual orientation:

Lover/s:

Unique traits or habits:

Anything else to remember?

Setting:

This is where and how your story takes place.

Is your story in the country or big city?

Is there a weather event? Snow, rain, heat?

In what country is your story set? What state? Is the area wealthy, poor, or a combination of both?

I write where I know so my stories to date have been set in New Jersey. I am currently working on a novel set elsewhere in the country, which brings more challenges. Only you can decide how deep you want to get with geographical and setting descriptions. If you are writing about a setting you don't know much about, research it first. If I read a novel that gets the setting wrong I am totally turned off.

Fiction Book Worksheet

My compelling WHY is:

Genre:

Viewpoint:

Main character:

Conflict character/s:

Supporting characters:

_____

_____

_____

Write a short paragraph: The main conflict of the story is :

_____

_____

_____

_____

_____

_____

_____

_____

Is there is a subplot (minor storyline going on throughout the book?

Subplot conflict is:

_____

_____

Setting:

I love to introduce weather aspects in my books. Many favorite books I've read have some type of weather, such as wind, rain, snow, cold or extreme heat, that has added another great element of suspense into the setting.

Setting of book:

Weather aspect:

Graphic or not graphic?

Sex, bondage or making love?

There are some other considerations to think about before writing a book. I did a lot of thinking before I wrote my books about how graphic I wanted them to be.

In the Simple Case series I let my imagination go wild. Nothing was off limits and there are graphic sex and murder scenes. When I hear that someone's mother read the book, I always think, "Yikes!" Always feel comfortable with what you are writing. Once it is in print there is no going back!

Graphic or not graphic:

| |
| |

Fiction Book - Putting it all together

Working title:

_____

Formatting

Paperback book size:

_____

Font:'

_____

Font Size:

_____

Word count:

_____

Page count:

_____

<u>Margins:</u>

Top:

Inside:

Gutter:

Bottom:

Outside:

Gutter Position:

Portrait

Mirror margins - apply whole document

Paragraph & Indentations and Spacing:

Alignment:

```



```

Outline:

```


```

Indentations:

Left:

```



```

Right:

```



```

Spacing:

Spacing Before:

```



```

Spacing After:

```



```

Special first line:

Line spacing:

Chapter Eleven

Publishing Choices and Scams

SCAMS

There are many publishing companies, independent agents and literary agencies out there and just as many scam artists ready to take your money.

Writer Beware:

An amazing resource I have used to research publishing companies, literary agents and self-publishing services is an online site called Writer Beware.

http://www.sfwa.org/for-authors/writer-beware/

This site will tell you everything you need to know about self-publishing services. It will tell you who has great reviews and who is out to scam you and take your money.

Publishing Options

The following services are free if you do the editing, formatting, and cover creation yourself:

Paperback - your choice of size.

1. Create Space - owned by Amazon.com.

Free, but they also offer a paid service to help with editing, formatting, and cover creation.

This company also offers a way to publish to Kindle.

eBooks.

2. KDP or Kindle Direct Publishing   owned by Amazon.com

I use page breaks to start each new chapter, which works well on Kindle.

3. Barnes & Noble Press: (formerly known as Nook Press & Pubit) owned by Barnes & Noble

With Nook I use section breaks rather than page breaks for a quality look. This is something unique to Nook.

4. Kobo writing life:

This is a newer self-publishing platform. It is free and I found it easy to use.

Again, I use page breaks on this publishing platform.

I may use the following free publishing choices:

1.
2.
3.
4.

To make eCovers I can use:

1.
2.
3.

When I first starting writing I had no idea about self-publishing. After much research I decided to use a publishing company called Infinity Publishing.

Infinity is a print on demand (POD) company. You give them your formatted manuscript; they create a cover and publish it on Amazon, Barnes & Noble, Buy Books On the Web, and other sites. They own the rights to the book cover.

I think the price is reasonable, but they take a chunk of your royalties and you do all the publicity for the book. They also were the only company I had found that pays a small royalty when you purchase your own books. I enjoyed my time with Infinity and if you want to start out with a POD company I feel good recommending them.

As I became more experienced I decided to take control of my authorship and book creation and publish my books myself on Kindle, Create Space, Kobo, and Barnes & Noble Press. I am always on the lookout for more sites to self publish. If you don't mind doing the work yourself and want to cut costs, Create Space, Kindle Direct Publishing, and Barnes & Noble Press are great sites to consider.

I will research the following print on demand companies.

1.	
2.	
3.	
4.	

My research shows that the best company for me to use is

For the following reasons:

1.	
2.	
3.	

The cost for my book will be:

This cost will include the following:

1.
2.
3.
4.
5.
6.

Any other considerations:

Chapter Twelve

Marketing your book:

Once your books are uploaded you'll need a marketing plan.

Free Marketing

1. Selling your book yourself on your own website

Many authors sell their books on their own websites as a way of keeping all the profits.

You can research designers or if you are tech savvy you can do it yourself.

2. Press Releases:

Sending a press_release to local newspapers is easy to do because many let you submit a story and photo online.

Issue a press release about me and my book by:

I have issued a press release to the following papers:

1.	
2.	
3.	
4.	
5.	
6.	

3. Word of mouth:

Tell your family, friends, co-workers, and acquaintances about your book. Have a copy ready to show them and be prepared to make a sale.

Ask them to tell their friends, family, and co-workers about your book.

4. Social Networking:

Social Networking is a must to get your name and book out there.

Let your friends and family know about your book by creating Facebook, Twitter, and Google + accounts.

LinkedIn is also a great place to post, but in a professional businesslike manner. Make sure you keep with the tone and messaging of each social media site.

<u>Facebook:</u>

I have created a page for my books and publishing business and post regularly. You can also add an email app to your fan/business page to collect email addresses for your newsletters. You first must create a personal page. Then log out until you are on the initial Facebook page. In the lower right corner you will see "Create a page for celebrity, band or business." Click there to create your fan page.

You can also sign up for google+, twitter, instagram and more!

Posting out on social media:

Warning! Do not over do this! People want to connect with you and get to know you on social media. They do not want to be sold to or see 50 posts a day about your book. I made this mistake early on because I was so excited about my books and I am sure it turned many people off.

Paid Marketing Ideas

1. Radio Commercials:

I did my own commercial for a local radio station. It was a really fun process and every night I would sit by the radio listening until it played. It was exciting to hear myself on the radio talking about "A Simple Case of Suicide." Unfortunately, it did not generate sales and wasn't worth the price for the commercial. Still, it was fun, and if I have spare cash I would do it again.

2. Bookstores:

Local bookstore are usually happy to carry your books. You will have to provide them and you will need to make sure you are getting a reasonable cut of the sales. The usual is 60% to you and 40% to the bookstore.

3. Giveaways:

Giving away something for free is another way I got my name out there and started to build a mailing list.

(On http://expertswritingacademy.mykajabi.com visitors opt-in for my free giveaway which is currently - The Four P's to Publication (as a pdf document with video training.) Make sure when you obtain email addresses you let the people know that they' re signing up to be on your mailing list. It is best to use a double opt in and in the Europe new rules are in place so be sure to read up on them before you create one. The larger the list, the more people you can notify when your next book comes out. There is a saying that the money is in the list. The more people you have signed up for your book releases or newsletter, the more sales you will make...hopefully!

4. Advertising:

Facebook and Google ads are great ways to get your product in front of people. Facebook does not offer phone support and I have found their email support to be slow, sometimes days before a response.

Google ads are something I have yet to figure out, but they do offer free support and will assign an ad specialist (for free at this time) to help you with designing and implementing your advertisement.

There are some websites and companies that offer Facebook and Google ad coupons.

Tip: Paid advertising - If you are placing an advertisement make sure you know up front how much it will cost so you can plan your budget accordingly. Don't miss something in the fine print and wind up paying more than you expected. Proceed here at your own risk. For online advertising, I highly recommend you research how to set your ad budget, length of ad run, pay per click vs. pay for impression.

I have found that Facebook has limited e-mail help, but will get back to you in time.

I will research and decide if I want to do an ad for my book. Where I will advertise?

The costs:

Ad 1
Ad 2
Ad 3
Ad 4

My budget:

| |
| |

Lifetime budget of each advertisement

| Ad 1 |
| Ad 2 |
| Ad 3 |
| Ad 4 |

How long will the ad run:

| Ad 1 |
| Ad 2 |
| Ad 3 |
| Ad 4 |

***Don't do an online or print advertisement until you know exactly how much it will cost!!!!

Putting it all together

Steps to market your book:

1. Create a personal Facebook page.

2. Create Facebook fan page linked to my personal page.

The name of my Facebook fan page is:

3. Create a Twitter account to let my friends and family know about your book.

My Twitter name is:

4. Create a Google + page. Every time you post or plus one it shows up on Google search engines.

My Google + page is:

<u>Local Bookstores</u> - It never hurts to ask your local bookstore to sell your book. Sometimes this is a losing proposition for the self-published writer, so always get a contract that stipulates the number of books they will carry and how much they will take from each sale.

My local bookstores are:

1.
2.
3.

<u>Giveaways</u> - Giveaways are something you can give away for free, such as an online report, to attract people to my book.

My ideas for giveaways are:

Commenting on other author's blogs:

It used to be that simply posting comments to get your name out there worked. In this new age of people constantly being bombarded online you need to be engaging and provide real content. The days of posting your name and book link are over.

I will comment and provide real insights on the following blogs. You can include a link to you books page on amazon.com, barnesandnoble.com or your own website, but don't overdo it!

1.
2.
3.
4.
5.

<u>Your own website:</u>

There are many companies that will design a website for you and the cost ranges from cheap to astronomical.

Be sure to know all the costs up front before and check out the quality of work before you hire a web designer.

Most authors have their own website and it can be a simple one pager or a flashy site with many pages. It is your choice!

I will research the following hosts if I am using Word Press.

1.
2.
3.

I will research other companies/designers that can assist me or build a website.

1.
2.
3.
4.

Chapter Thirteen

By now you should have a pretty good idea of where to begin your exciting writing adventure. I hope you have enjoyed this book and the exercises in it.

Remember:

Kick your inner critic to the curb and pick up that pen, pencil, or keyboard.

I believe in you and I know you can do it!

Don't forget to sign up for The Four P's to Publication pdf and video training at expertswritingacademy.mykajabi.com

You will find an opportunity to join our eCourse with lessons taken directly from this book.

Until we meet again. Love with an open and accepting heart - starting with yourself first. Celebrate your victories, no matter how small and never stop believing and going for your dreams!

Happy Writing!

Laura J. Kendall, CPC

Author & Founder of Experts Writing Academy.

You can connect with me at:

www.expertswritingacademy.com

www.authorlaurajkendall.com

amazon.com/author/laurajkendall

Don't forget to check out our online training for writing and publishing your book at expertsacademy.mykajabi.com

Notes

Notes

www.ingramcontent.com/pod-product-compliance
Lightning Source LLC
Chambersburg PA
CBHW081656270326
41933CB00017B/3191